W9-AMV-822

AWESOME VALUES IN FAMOUS LIVES

Lance Armstrong

Determined to Beat the Odds

Barbara Kramer

Enslow Elementary
an imprint of
Enslow Publishers, Inc.

40 Industrial Road   PO Box 38
Box 398   Aldershot
Berkeley Heights, NJ 07922   Hants GU12 6BP
USA   UK

http://www.enslow.com

Enslow Elementary, an imprint of Enslow Publishers, Inc.

Enslow Elementary® is a registered trademark of Enslow Publishers, Inc.

Library of Congress Cataloging-in-Publication Data

Lance Armstrong : determined to beat the odds / Barbara Kramer.
    p. cm. — (Awesome values in famous lives)
    Includes bibliographical references and index.
    ISBN 0-7660-2377-X (hardcover)
    1. Armstrong, Lance—Juvenile literature. 2. Cyclists—United States-Biography—Juvenile literature.
3. Cancer—Patients—United States—Biography—Juvenile literature. I. Title. II. Series.
GV1051.A76K73 2005
796.6'2'092—dc22

                                           2004004505

Printed in the United States of America

10 9 8 7 6 5 4 3 2 1

To Our Readers: We have done our best to make sure all Internet Addresses in this book were active and appropriate when we went to press. However, the author and the publisher have no control over and assume no liability for the material available on those Internet sites or on other Web sites they may link to. Any comments or suggestions can be sent by e-mail to comments@enslow.com or to the address on the back cover.

Every effort has been made to locate all copyright holders of material used in this book. If any errors or omissions have occurred, corrections will be made in future editions of this book.

Illustration Credits: AP/Wide World, pp. 2, 4, 6, 8, 12, 13, 14, 16, 17, 18, 19, 20, 22, 23, 25, 26, 29, 30, 31, 32 (all), 34, 35, 36, 38, 39, 40, 41, 42, 43; Courtesy of Bending Oaks High School, p. 10; Jerry Startt, p. 28; Linda Armstrong Kelly, pp. 7, 9.

Cover illustration: AP/Wide World.

Contents

Lance Armstrong

CHAPTER 1

Finding His Sport

Lance Armstrong smiled and waved as he pedaled his bicycle in Paris, France, on July 25, 2004. Thousands of people lined the street, all cheering and shouting. Lance had done it again. He had won the Tour de France bicycle race.

The Tour de France is a very hard race. It takes three weeks and covers more than two thousand miles. The bikers twist and turn through the city and the country. They pedal up steep mountain roads. Some people say the Tour de France is the hardest sporting event in the world. Winning it once is terrific. But Lance has won it six times—something no one else has done. That was amazing, especially for Lance.

Eight years earlier, in 1996, Lance was fighting for his life. He had a serious illness called cancer. He worried about his future. Would he ever be strong enough to race again? Lance was determined to beat the illness and get back on his bicycle.

Lance was born on September 18, 1971, and grew up in Plano, Texas.

Lance won the Tour de France six times!

His parents split up when he was a toddler. With just the two of them, Lance and his mother grew very close. She married again when Lance was three, but that marriage ended when Lance was a teenager. Then Lance and his mother, Linda Armstrong, were on their own again.

Lance's mom was always his biggest fan.

Lance liked sports, but it took a while to find his favorite one. He tried football but was not good at it. When he was in fifth grade, he tried running. Winning a race made Lance feel great. After that, he ran more races on the weekends.

Lance wanted to swim, too, but he had a lot to learn. At first, the coach put Lance, who was twelve,

Lance's Busy Day

1. Bike ten miles to the pool.
2. Swim from 5:30 a.m. to 7 a.m.
3. Go to school.
4. Swim for two more hours.
5. Bike ten miles home.

into a class with kids who were only seven. Looking around, he saw his friend's little sister. "It was embarrassing," Lance said.[1] But he did not give up. Instead, he worked even harder, and soon he was winning races against boys his own age.

Everyone on the team had to swim six miles every day. In the mornings, Lance rode his bike to the pool for swim team practice. After school, the swim team had another workout.

When Lance was thirteen, he entered a race called the Iron Kids triathlon. The race had three parts: swimming, biking, and running. Lance came in first, even though he was racing against bigger kids.

When he entered another triathlon, he won that one, too. Soon Lance's mother was driving him to races all over Texas. She told Lance always to do his best and keep trying. "You can't quit . . . ," she said. "Even if you have to walk to the finish line."[2]

By the time he was sixteen, Lance was making about $20,000 a year in prize money in triathlons.

"I'm going to be a champ," Lance told his mom.[3]

It seemed as if nothing could stop him. One time he got hit by a car while he was riding his bike. He sprained his knee and cut his head and his foot. The doctor told him to rest for three weeks. Lance could not sit still that long. Six days later, he competed in a triathlon and came in third place.

As a teen, Lance focused all his energy on sports.

After racing in more triathlons, Lance decided to give up swimming and running. "I looked at what I did best, what I liked best," he said.[4] That was cycling. Lance had found his sport. Lance graduated from Bending Oaks High School in 1989. He had no plans for college. He knew that his future was in sports.

CHAPTER 2

Cycling Pro

Europeans love bicycling as much as Americans love baseball. So, for a cyclist, Europe is the place to go. In 1990, Lance moved to Austin, Texas—but he spent much of his time racing his bicycle in Europe. At first, Lance raced to gain more experience. He was on a team that trained cyclists to become professionals. For professionals, racing is their job.

Bike racing is a team sport. Each team of nine riders has a leader. The rest of the riders are all trying to help their leader win the race. Some cyclists on the team protect their leader. To do this, they ride jammed tightly together in a pack. This keeps other teams' riders from bumping into the leader and knocking him down.

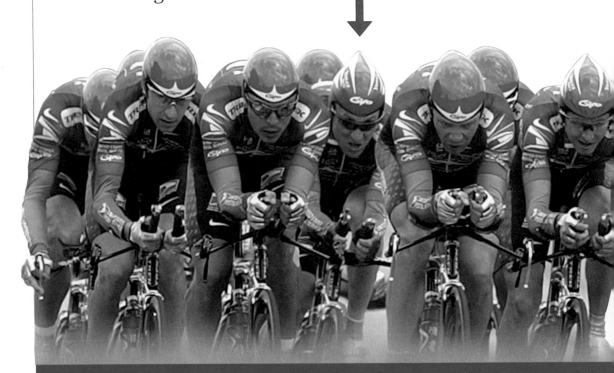

Lance is riding in the middle of the pack
so his teammates can protect him.

Some team members ride in front of their leader to block the wind. This helps the leader save his energy, because riding into the wind is harder. When the time is right, the leader moves ahead of the pack and rides his fastest to the finish line.

At first, Lance was a team member, trying to help his leader win. But he was being trained to become a team leader. Lance spent five or six hours a day on his bike, either training or racing. His hard work brought results. In 1991, he won the U.S. Amateur Championship.

In 1992, Lance was one of three cyclists chosen to race on the U.S. Olympic Team in Barcelona, Spain. When Lance finished in fourteenth place, he was not happy. He had hoped to win. Still, the director of a professional team saw Lance's skill. He invited Lance to join the Motorola team.

Lance's first race as a pro—or professional—was in San Sebastian, Spain. On that cold and rainy day, the roads were wet and dangerously slick. The slower riders began dropping out of the race. But Lance was determined to finish. "It was raining so hard it hurt," he said. "But I had to finish."[1]

Lance became a professional athlete on the Motorola team.

Lance pedaled along in the rain, even though he was far behind the other riders. Some people booed as he crossed the finish line. Lance felt awful. "I thought maybe I wasn't any good," he said.[2] Should he give up racing?

Of the 111 cyclists racing in Spain that day, Lance ended up in last place.

No. Lance refused to be a quitter. He kept working hard, and in his next race, he finished in second place.

In 1993, in his first full season as a pro, Lance won ten events. Three of them were important one-day races in the United States. Lance was given an extra $1 million for winning all three races. He split the money with his team members.

In July 1993, Lance entered the Tour de France. A *tour*, also known as a *stage race*, lasts for many days

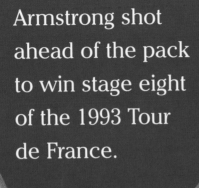

Armstrong shot ahead of the pack to win stage eight of the 1993 Tour de France.

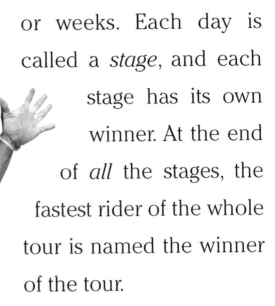

or weeks. Each day is called a *stage*, and each stage has its own winner. At the end of *all* the stages, the fastest rider of the whole tour is named the winner of the tour.

Riders in the Tour de France race almost every day for three weeks. It is a long, hard race, even for skilled cyclists. "I'm here to learn, really," Lance said.[3] Then he surprised everyone by winning a stage on the eighth day of the race. A few days

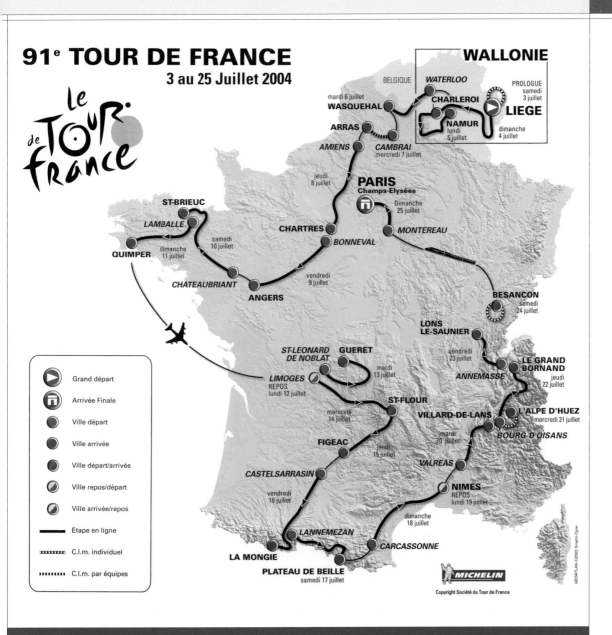

91ᵉ TOUR DE FRANCE
3 au 25 Juillet 2004

le Tour de France

WALLONIE

BELGIQUE

WATERLOO

PROLOGUE
samedi
3 juillet

mardi 6 juillet
WASQUEHAL

CHARLEROI

LIEGE

ARRAS

NAMUR
lundi
5 juillet

dimanche
4 juillet

AMIENS

CAMBRAI
mercredi 7 juillet

jeudi
8 juillet

PARIS
Champs-Elysées

Dimanche
25 juillet

ST-BRIEUC

MONTEREAU

LAMBALLE

CHARTRES

samedi
10 juillet

dimanche
11 juillet

BONNEVAL

QUIMPER

BESANCON
samedi
24 juillet

vendredi
9 juillet

CHATEAUBRIANT

ANGERS

LONS
LE-SAUNIER

ST-LEONARD
DE NOBLAT

GUERET

LE GRAND
BORNAND

mardi
13 juillet

vendredi
23 juillet

jeudi
22 juillet

LIMOGES
REPOS
lundi 12 juillet

ANNEMASSE

ST-FLOUR

L'ALPE D'HUEZ
mercredi 21 juillet

mercredi
14 juillet

VILLARD-DE-LANS

BOURG-D'OISANS

FIGEAC

mardi
20 juillet

jeudi
15 juillet

VALREAS

CASTELSARRASIN

NIMES
REPOS
lundi 19 juillet

vendredi
16 juillet

dimanche
18 juillet

LANNEMEZAN

CARCASSONNE

LA MONGIE

PLATEAU DE BEILLE
samedi 17 juillet

MICHELIN

Copyright Société du Tour de France

GEOATLAS-©2003 Graph-Ogre

Légende

▶ Grand départ
🏛 Arrivée Finale
● Ville départ
● Ville arrivée
● Ville départ/arrivée
◐ Ville repos/départ
◐ Ville arrivée/repos
— Etape en ligne
xxxxxxx C.l.m. individuel
········· C.l.m. par équipes

The Tour de France changes every year.
This map shows the route for 2004.

Lance crossed the finish line to win in Norway in 1993.

later, his coach pulled him out of the tour. Most riders do not finish their first Tour de France. Lance was not yet strong enough, or fast enough, to finish the whole race.

In August 1993 Lance competed in the World Championships in Oslo, Norway. It was another cold, rainy day. Lance crashed twice on the slippery streets. But he did not give up. He climbed back on his bike and kept riding.

Lance was in fourth place as the cyclists neared the end of the race. Then he attacked. He pedaled as hard as he could to break away from the pack. He zoomed ahead on his bike and finished in first place. Lance was the new world champion.

The king shares a laugh with Lance.

After winning the World Championships in Oslo in 1993, Lance was invited to meet King Harald V of Norway. When Lance and his mother came to the palace, his mother was told to wait outside. Lance's mother had been his biggest fan ever since he was a kid. He would not leave her behind—even to meet a king.

"Come on, let's go," he said to his mother.[4] As they walked away, a guard ran after them. The king said he would meet both of them. Lance and his mother went inside, where the king awarded Lance a gold medal.

On this steep mountain road, Lance rides in the lead.

CHAPTER 3

Honoring a Friend

Lance kept on learning more about racing. In 1994 he again rode in some stages of the Tour de France. In 1995 he set a higher goal. This time, he planned to finish the whole race. He also wanted to win one of the stages.

Stage fifteen of the race took riders on a steep climb through the mountains. Lance was

Lance, in yellow, is at the front of the pack
on this road in southern France.

speeding downhill when he saw some cyclists lying
on the road. He was going too fast to see what had
happened.

After the race, Lance got bad news. His teammate Fabio Casartelli had crashed into a cement
wall. Fabio died from his injuries. It was a sad day
for the Motorola team. No one felt much like racing,

and they talked about quitting the Tour de France. Then they decided that it would honor Fabio more to finish the race in his memory.

Lance points to the heavens in memory of Fabio, who died during the race.

Three days later, Lance and twelve other riders were ahead of everyone else. Near the top of a mountain, Lance took the lead. The chase was on as other cyclists worked hard to catch up.

With eighteen miles left in the stage, Lance was tired, but he did not stop. "I was very, very bad in the last bit," Lance said, "but I kept thinking of him."[1] As he crossed the finish line, Lance pointed to the sky. This win was for Fabio.

Racing Manners

People in Europe were saying that Lance was a show-off. They did not like the way he pumped his fists into the air when he won a race. They said he always bragged when he talked to reporters. They thought it was rude to act that way.

Lance wanted to be liked in Europe. So he learned to mind his manners. When he won a race, he celebrated later, away from the crowds. Soon people in Europe were talking about his good riding, instead of his bad manners.

Lance got off to a great start in 1996. He won two races and took second place in six races. But he did not do well in the Tour de France. After a day of racing in the rain, he was sick and coughing all the time. "I couldn't breathe," he said.[2] He had to drop out of the Tour de France after only five stages.

Lance's next race was at the 1996 Olympics Games in Atlanta, Georgia. Thousands of Americans cheered him on. They were sure that Lance would win. But he was feeling tired. When it came time to race hard to the finish line, Lance could not do it.

He had run out of steam. He ended up in twelfth place.

In September 1996, Lance was asked to join the Cofidis team, a racing team from France. He would be making $2 million dollars. That month Lance turned twenty-five. He invited his friends and family to his house for a big birthday party.

A few days later, Lance coughed up blood. He also had terrible headaches. After some tests, the doctor gave Lance

Lance did poorly in the Olympic Games in 1996. What was going on?

bad news. He had cancer. It had spread to many parts of his body, even into his brain.

For Lance, everything suddenly changed. Bicycle racing no longer seemed important. He was terribly ill, and he knew that he could die. "I just wanted to make it to my twenty-sixth birthday," he said.[3]

In 1996 the cycling champ faced the hardest race of his life—the race to beat cancer.

CHAPTER 4

The Fight of His Life

Lance had an operation to remove two tumors from his brain. Then he needed twelve weeks of treatments with cancer-fighting drugs. The drugs are strong, and they make patients feel very sick.

When he could, Lance rode his bike. He was weak, but that did not matter. "I just want to be on my bike, outside, with my friends," he said.[1]

Lance had his last treatment in December 1996. By then he had made a decision. He wanted to reach out to other people with cancer. In January 1997, he started the Lance Armstrong Foundation. It would raise money for research to prevent and cure cancer. While Lance was working on a project for his foundation, he met Kristin Richard. She was helping with the plans. They had fun working together, and soon they began dating.

Lance was feeling better, but doctors

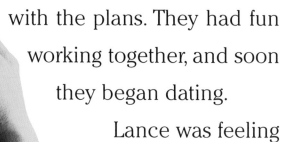

The drugs that cured Lance's cancer made his hair fall out for a while.

said he should not race in 1997. During his time off he golfed, fished, and worked at home on his yard. He also spent time riding his bike and lifting weights to get strong again.

In the fall of 1997, the doctors said Lance's cancer was all gone. He was ready to return to bicycle racing. But the Cofidis team did not want him anymore. They thought he would not be strong enough to be a team leader.

Lance started a program called *Cycle of Hope* to teach people about cancer.

Lance talked to other teams, but they all said no. It seemed that no one believed he would be able to race again. Finally, Lance found a place on the United States Postal Service Cycling Team. It was the only team that would give him a chance.

Could Lance still lead a team to victory?

In February 1998 Lance rode in his first race of the season. It was a five-day race in Spain. He finished in fourteenth place, and he was not happy. "I was used to leading, not finishing fourteenth," he said.[2]

Two weeks later, he rode in an eight-day race in France. The second day was cold, windy, and rainy. It drained Lance's energy, and he pulled out of the race. He went home to Texas feeling tired and sad.

"I didn't unpack my bike for four weeks," he said.[3] Then a couple of friends asked him to ride with them in North Carolina. They spent long days biking in the mountains. Lance had plenty of time to think. By the end of the trip, he was ready to race again.

In May 1988, Lance married Kristin Richard. Then they left for Europe, where Lance rode in several races. He won the four-day Tour of Luxembourg and placed fourth in the Tour of Holland. He came in fourth in the Tour of Spain, a difficult twenty-three-day race. Then he placed fourth in the World Championships. By the end of the season, Lance had a new goal. He wanted to win the Tour de France.

In the Tour de France, cyclists must ride up
and down mountains in rain and shine.

CHAPTER 5

Winning Again

Lance worked hard to get ready for the 1999 Tour de France. He biked each stage of the race over and over again. He wanted to practice on every curve and hill so he would be able to ride his fastest.

The first stage of the Tour de France is a short race. Each rider is timed to see how fast he crosses the finish line. The fastest rider gets to

Lance's mom was very proud of him during the 1999 Tour de France.

wear a special yellow shirt and start at the front of the pack for stage two.

Lance won the first stage in 1999, so he began stage two in the yellow shirt and riding at the front. Two days later, Lance fell to second place. He had to give up the yellow shirt and the front starting place. On stage eight, Lance again gained the lead—and he did not lose it again.

On July 25, 1999, Lance Armstrong became the second American to win the Tour de France. It was the first time the winner was part of an American team. In 1986 an American, Greg LeMond, had won the tour, but he was riding with a French team.

A few months later, in October 1999, Lance and Kristin celebrated the birth of their son, Luke. Then Lance went back to work, riding his bike three hundred to six hundred miles every week. A victory in one Tour de France was not enough for Lance. He wanted to win again.

In 2000, Lance won his second Tour de France. He also earned a bronze medal

After the 2000 Tour de France, Luke wore a tiny yellow shirt—just like Dad's.

The town of Austin, Texas, held a parade in honor
of Lance's history-making comeback.

for being the third-place winner at the 2000 Summer Olympic Games in Sydney, Australia.

In July 2001, Lance won the Tour de France for the third time in a row. That fall, his twin daughters, Isabelle and Grace, were born.

Could anyone ever beat Lance? After his fourth win, in the 2002 Tour de France, it did not seem possible. A year later, Lance faced his most challenging tour yet. During the 2003 Tour de France, he struggled with one problem after another.

King of the Mountain

What is Lance's secret for winning? He trains hard all year-round, even in bad weather. One day he was training in the mountains of southern France. The mountain stretched 4,978 feet into the air, and the road climbed seven and a half miles. It was very cold and raining hard.

At the top of the mountain, his coach was waiting in a warm car to give Lance a ride home. But Lance would not go. "I don't think I got it. I don't understand it," he said. Lance wanted to know every twist and turn of the road. So he biked down the mountain and then climbed it again.[1]

Sometimes the cheering fans get in the way. They crowd in too close to the cyclists.

First he was sick with a stomach flu. Next, on a day when temperatures climbed to 104 degrees Fahrenheit, he ran out of water. Athletes need to drink lots of water. Without it, Lance felt weak and had trouble finishing the stage.

He also fell twice during the tour. The second time his handlebars had gotten tangled up with the strap of a fan's bag. Even so, Lance overcame all those problems to win his fifth Tour de France.

Lance fell twice but still claimed the victory
in the 2003 Tour de France.

Lance's family greeted him at the finish line in Paris.
They flashed five fingers for his fifth win.

A few months after the 2003 Tour de France,
Lance and Kristin announced that they were getting
a divorce.

In 2004, Lance became the first cyclist in
the world to win the Tour de France six times.

Thousands of fans cheered for Lance as he rode toward the finish line. Many of them were wearing a yellow wristband with the words "LIVE STRONG."[2]

Millions of these wristbands have been sold all around the world. The money goes to the Lance Armstrong Foundation. It is for programs to help young people with cancer.

Winning the Tour de France six times has made Lance rich and famous. But he has said that beating cancer is his greatest victory. Doctors had told Lance that he might not live, but Lance beat the odds. Now he wants his wins in the Tour de France to give hope to others who are fighting a deadly illness. "Every time I win another Tour, I prove that I'm alive—and . . . that others can survive, too," he said.[3]

"I hope to win one more Tour de France,"
said Lance in 2005.[4]

Timeline

1971 Lance is born on September 18.

1984 Wins the Iron Kids triathlon.

1989 Graduates from Bending Oaks High School in Dallas, Texas.

1992 Begins his professional cycling career.

1996 Learns that he has cancer, and it has spread to many parts of his body.

1997 Starts the Lance Armstrong Foundation.

1998 Marries Kristin Richard on May 8 (they divorce in 2003).

1999 His son, Luke, is born.

2001 His twin daughters, Isabelle and Grace, are born.

1999–2003 Wins the Tour de France five years in a row.

2004 Becomes the first person to win the Tour de France six times.

2005 Announces that he will retire from professional cycling after the 2005 Tour de France.

Words to Know

amateur—Someone who does a sport or other activity for fun or to gain experience.

cancer—A group of diseases in which cells in or on the body become abnormal and grow out of control. Without treatment, these cells can destroy healthy parts of the body.

charity—Giving money or other help to those in need.

foundation—An organization created to give money for research, education, and to help people in need.

professional—Someone who does a sport or other activity as a job.

research—Studying something to learn more about it.

triathlon—A race that has three parts: swimming, bicycling, and running.

Chapter Notes

CHAPTER 1.
Finding His Sport

1. Lance Armstrong with Sally Jenkins, *It's Not About the Bike: My Journey Back to Life* (New York: The Berkley Publishing Group, 2001 edition), p. 22.

2. Ibid., p. 28.

3. Ibid., p. 21.

4. Leigh Montville, "Breaking Away," *Sports Illustrated*, July 4, 1994, p. 54.

CHAPTER 2.
Cycling Pro

1. Geoff Drake, "America's Lone Star," *Bicycling*, May 1993, p. 66.

2. Samuel Abt, *Lance Armstrong's Comeback from Cancer* (San Francisco: Vander Plas Publications, 2000), p. 24.

3. Samuel Abt, "On Fast Wheels to a Bright Future," *New York Times*, July 5, 1993, p. 32.

4. Lance Armstrong with Sally Jenkins, *It's Not About the Bike: My Journey Back to Life* (New York: The Berkley Publishing Group, 2001 edition), p. 62.

CHAPTER 3.
Honoring a Friend

1. Samuel Abt, "Teammate's Death Inspires Armstrong to Win Stage of Tour," *The New York Times*, July 22, 1995, p. 27.

2. Samuel Abt, "An Ailing Armstrong Drops Out of Race," *New York Times*, July 6, 1996, p. 27.

3. Stacey Schultz and Linda Kulman, "Racing for the Cure," *U.S. News & World Report*, August 9, 1999, p. 60.

CHAPTER 4.
The Fight of His Life

1. Samuel Abt, "Armstrong Acknowledges Cancer Battle," *New York Times*, October 9, 1996, p. B16.

2. Lance Armstrong with Sally Jenkins, *It's Not About the Bike: My Journey Back to Life* (New York: The Berkley Publishing Group, 2001 edition), p. 184.

3. Frank Litsky, "Ultimate Overachiever: Lance Edward Armstrong," *New York Times*, July 26, 1999, p. D4.

CHAPTER 5.
Winning Again

1. Michael Hall, "Lance Armstrong Has Something to Get Off His Chest," *Texas Monthly*, July 2001, p. 70.

2. "Lance, Back from France," *People*, August 30, 2004, p. 64.

3. Lance Armstrong with Sally Jenkins, *Every Second Counts* (New York: Broadway Books, 2003), p. 3.

4. "Armstrong to Quit After 2005 Tour," CNN online, April 18, 2005.

Learn More

Armstrong, Kristin. *Lance Armstrong: The Race of His Life.* New York: Grosset & Dunlap, 2000.

Bradley, Michael. *Lance Armstrong.* New York: Benchmark Books, 2005.

Christopher, Matt. *On the Bike With . . . Lance Armstrong.* New York: Little, Brown, 2003.

Donovan, Sandy. *Lance Armstrong.* Minneapolis, Minn.: Lerner, 2005.

Stewart, Mark. *Sweet Victory: Lance Armstrong's Incredible Journey.* Brookfield, Conn.: Millbrook, 2000.

Internet Addresses

Lance Armstrong Online includes his biography and a photo gallery.

<http://lancearmstrong.com>

The official Fan Club of Lance Armstrong and the Discovery Channel Pro Cycling Team

<http://thepaceline.com>

Index

 (decorative)